Giovanna Magi

LISBON

SINTRA - QUELUZ - CASCAIS - ESTORIL

SERIES '90 - NEW EDITION

BONECHI

© Copyright 1992 by
CASA EDITRICE BONECHI
Via Cairoli 18/b
50131 Firenze
Telex 571323 CEB
Fax 55/5000766

Exclusive distributor:
EDITORIAL SOFOTO, LDA.
Rua Eça de Queiroz
Lote 42-Chesol-Aldeia de Juso
2750 Cascais - Portugal
Tel. 285 15 05

Printed in E.E.C. by
Centro Stampa Editoriale Bonechi

PHOTO FROM THE ARCHIVES OF
CASA EDITRICE BONECHI, TAKEN
BY:

Luigi Di Giovine, pages 23-31, 35, 37a,
38a, 39, 45b, 49, 52, 53, 56, 57, 59.

Jean-Charles Pinheira, pages 1, 4, 5a, 6,
19a, 20b, 33, 35, 37b, 41, 50, 51, 54, 55a,
58, 62.

EDITORIAL SOFOTO

Marcelo Dau, pages: Cover, 5b, 7-14, 18,
19b, 20a, 22, 32, 40, 42, 44, 45a,c, 46-48,
60, 61.

Chester Brummel, pages: 15-17, 21, 24,
36, 38b, 43, 55b, 63.

A BRIEF HISTORY OF THE CITY

THE CITY'S ORIGINS

According to an existing legend Lisbon was founded by Ulysses during his wanderings, and indeed for a long time the city was known as Ulyssipona. *Historians, on the other hand, claim that city's origins go back to 1200 B.C. when it was a Phoenician colony called* Alis Ubo, *literally " quiet port ". Conquered first by Greece and later by Carthage, in 205 B.C. Lisbon became a Roman city and was renamed* Felicitas Julia *in honor of Julius Caesar. Thereafter it was invaded by barbarians who reinforced the city walls. In 711 the city fell into the hands of the Arabs and remained under Arab rule for four hundred years. With the name of* Lissabona *it blossomed into a splendid commercial center. Then during a terrible storm in the summer of 1147 several ships carrying Crusaders of the Second Crusade on their way to the Holy Land were forced to anchor along the coast near the city of Porto. The Crusaders, of Flemish, German, and English nationalities, offered their services to King Afonso Henriques I who wished to drive the Arab conquerors out of the city. After a four month long siege, the Arabs were defeated and in 1255 Afonso III set up his court in Lisbon, whereby Lisbon was chosen as the capital of the Kingdom.*

THE GOLDEN AGE

Lisbon's vertiginous rise began under João I the Great, founder of the Aviz dynasty. In no time at all, it became the wealthiest city in the whole Western world.
On July 8, 1497 Vasco da Gama, commanding a fleet of four ships, set sail from Lisbon on his way to the Indies. Sailing around the Cape of Good Hope by way of Mozambique, he reached Calicut, and thus the sea route to India was cleared! Soon afterwards in 1500 Pedro Alvares Cabral made another thrilling discovery: Brazil. And it was Camões, Portugal's greatest poet, who so splendidly extolled these exciting discoveries. With the advent of the Manuelian style typified by the use of motifs representing waves, corals, exotic animals, sea knots, and sea shells applied to the Gothic style, even architecture bowed to Lisbon's supremacy on the high seas. The ivory, silver, silks, spices, and gems flooding Lisbon's market-places found their way into the city's private homes, within the reach of one and all.

THE GREAT EARTHQUAKE

For two hundred years, during the 16th and 17th centuries, Lisbon, as well as the rest of Portugal, had been the greatest sea power in all of Europe: in fact, it was Lisbon itself which had caused the eclipse of mighty Genoa and Venice. Then, without warning, fate struck a cruel blow. On November 1, 1755 everyone was in church attending services as Solemn High Masses were being celebrated throughout the city for All Saints Day. All of a sudden a violent rumble shook the earth so hard that it actually rose up and was torn asunder a number of times. Churches, palaces, and monuments crumbled, burying everyone beneath the rubble. At the same time, the lit candles in the churches set fire to the hangings and furnishings inside and soon the whole city was aflame. People desperately seeking shelter along the banks of the Tagus River were instead greeted by death and destruction: a huge tidal wave broke the riverbanks and flooded the lower city swallowing in its wake not only the population, but also the wealth that had been Lisbon's glory for two centuries long. The king, José I, was unharmed only because he and his court were then lodged in Belém. Luckily, the man who would forge the tormented and destroyed city's triumphant rebirth was also part of the king's retinue: the royal minister and future Marquis of Pombal.

POMBAL'S LISBON

In the chaos which inevitably followed the catastrophe, Pombal did exactly what the situation called for: he brought aid to the wounded, had the dead buried, and ordered that the " vultures " caught preying on the population by robbing and sacking be punished with the death penalty. At the same time, working in collaboration with Manuel de Maia, a civil engineer, and Eugenio dos Santos, an architect, he drew up a plan to rebuild the city. Pombal's plan entailed razing the old houses and alleys of the lower city in order to carry out an urban renewal projet extremely modern for his times. The project included broad streets intersecting at right angles, flanked by buildings with harmoniously similar façades and mansard roofs embellished by wrought-iron balconies and lanterns. Moreover, the city would spread along the riverside. In remembrance of the terrible earthquake, one building, the Church of Carmo, was purposely left just as it looked on the fateful holiday morning: its lofty vaulting, ogival arches, and ample but gaping windows dominate the lovely square known as Rossio as living witness to that far-off day of tragedy.

LISBON TODAY

During the 19th century Lisbon was somewhat cut off from the rest of Europe, but this relative isolation lasted only a short while. In 1940 a world's fair held along the banks of the Tagus thrust the city once more into the world limelight.
Today Lisbon's airport is one of the most important air links connecting Europe and America and its port, with docks spread over more than 30 kilometers along that banks of the Tagus, is one of the biggest harbors in the world.
New buildings, entire neighborhoods and a fine university have sprung up. Lastly, in 1967, the April 25 Bridge, Europe's longest suspension bridge, was triumphantly completed, thus linking the banks of the Tagus.

ROSSIO

The name of this square, the most important in the Baixa quarter in the lower city, is officially called Praça Dom Pedro IV. In Portuguese, Rossio means the focal point, the city's meeting place and, in fact, the square is always throbbing with life far into the night. Its present appearance is the work of the Marquis of Pombal who bounded it on three sides with elegant buildings. The tasteful peristyle façade of the **Teatro Nacional Dona Maria II** opens into the north side of the square. It was put up between 1840 and 1846 by the Italian architect Fortunato Lodi on the site where the Palace of the Inquisition had once stood. On the façade there is a *statue of Gil Vicente,* the creator of the Portuguese theater. In the middle of the square stands a bronze statue of King Pedro IV (crowned Emperor of Brazil with the name of Pedro I). The sculpture is placed between two lovely Baroque fountains under which you can always see flower sellers whose colorful stalls brighten up the square.

PRAÇA DA FIGUEIRA

This square is adjacent to Rossio Square and it too is dominated by a statue, this one being an equestrian figure depicting João, King of Portugal. From this square, paved in an unusual black and white design, the Castle of São Jorge can be admired in all its grandeur as is majestically looms over the charming old houses seemingly crowded one on top of the other.

THE CATHEDRAL (Sé Patriarcal)

It was built at the end of the 12th century, as tradition would have it by the French architects Robert and Bernard who had previously designed the Cathedral of Coimbra. In fact, just like the Cathedral of Coimbra and also the Cathedrals of Evora and Oporto, the Cathedral of Lisbon had originally been a fortress erected for defensive purposes, as one can clearly tell from the sturdy towers on either side of the façade. The original Romanesque church underwent two reconstructions: one, in Gothic style, after the earthquake of 1344 and then another after the earthquake of 1755. This latter restoration returned the cathedral back to its original Romanesque style.

The façade with its twin towers opens into a spacious arch topped by a rose window. The interior, with single aisles and a transept, is characterized by tri-mullioned windows along the length of the nave and all along the transept.

THE SÃO JORGE CASTLE

Built by the Visigoths in the 5th century, it then became the residence of the Moors, up until the time it was modified by Afonso Henriques. The impression of might and majesty of the exterior is somewhat softened, once inside the passageway, at the sight of swans and white peacocks wandering peacefully about the green lawns.

For anyone who wishes to take in a view of incomparable beauty and at the same time get an unforgettable image of Lisbon forever

imprinted in his memory this is perhaps the finest spot of all. From the castle terrace, one's sight may freely rove all over the city spread out below and glide over the myriad rooftops until alighting upon the glistening loveliness of the " Sea of Straw ", as the Portuguese call the branch of the Tagus which here widens out until practically becoming ocean. The water as it is struck by the magic plays of sunlight suddenly takes on lovely golden reflections, just like the color of straw.

THE ALFAMA

Alfama is the oldest and quaintest quarter of Lisbon. Already in existence during Visigoth times, it extends around the Castle between the Church of São Vincente de Fora and the ocean. It is a maze of streets and alleyways which crisscross and crowd one another, with steep slopes and narrow flights of stairs unexpectedly coming out into tiny gardens. The houses, practically all dating back to the 16th century,

often have noteworthy façades which are either painted or decorated with azulejos tiles or else embellished by the lacework of a wrought–iron balcony. Life here flows on in peace and quiet, only interrupted now and again by the sudden cries of pushcart vendors, the strumming of a guitar, or the happy singing of a young girl. Night time in the Alfama quarter belongs totally to the " fado ". The fado, so typical an expression of the Portuguese culture, folk heritage, and spirit, is the kind of melancholy and haunting song which seems to have come right down from the love songs sung by the troubadors of the Middle Ages. As time went by, the fado took on sadder and sadder tones and, in time, to this mournfulness was added the sensuality of the Brazilian slave songs. The fado tells of love with its few joys and many sorrows, stressing the part fate plays (and, in fact, the word " fado " derives from the Latin " fatum "). It expresses, in its truest sense, a feeling just about untranslatable, called **saudade** which indicates that mixture of joy and touching melancholy that the fado conjures up in the Portuguese soul.

MIRADOURO DE SANTA LUZIA

A small square, a latticed terrace, flowering shrubs, and sunlight in patches here and there: from this spot one can admire Alfama's rainbow array of colors in all its splendor as it climbs up the hill in a forest of rooftops and daring perspectives. From up here one gets a fine view of the harbor and the Tagus's widening branch. In addition, the external walls of the *church of Santa Luzia,* located here in the square are covered all over with azulejo tiles, one of which shows how the Praça do Comércio originally looked.

CASA DOS BICOS

(The House of the Pointed Stones)

Built at the beginning of the 16th century, this house called dos Bicos (literally, of the promontory) stands out with unexpected brightness against the dark-colored houses of the Alfama quarter. Once, in this house with its characteristic façade of diamond-shaped stonework, lived the Albuquerque family.

THE CHURCH OF SÃO VICENTE DE FORA

The architect who designed this late Renaissance church was an Italian, Filippo Terzi, who built it between 1582 and 1627. The façade, preceded by a spacious flight of stairs leading up to it, is designed in two orders and flanked by bell towers. The interior, with side chapels and a transept and without aisles, is full of works dating from the Baroque period.

THE CHURCH OF SÃO VICENTE DE FORA
Monastery

The monastery's original refectory was turned into a Pantheon for the royal house of Braganza in 1855. The tombs of most of the dynasty's reigning monarchs are to be found here: from the first, Duke John of Braganza who took the title of João IV of Portugal, up to the last king who died in his London exile in 1932, Manuel II.

THE CHURCH OF SÃO VICENTE DE FORA
Porch

One of the most striking characteristics of the São Vicente monastery is that the walls of the porch are covered with splendid 18th century azulejo tiles depicting historical scenes, in large sizes. The cloister too is covered with azulejo tiles, this time illustrating scenes from La Fontaine's fables.
The azulejo is a painted or enameled terracotta tile of Moorish derivation. Its name comes from "azzulleig" and "azul," both of which indicate the blue which is the predominant color of the tiles. Lisbon was the main port of arrival in Europe for Chinese porcelains and thus her artistic production more than any other country's came under the influence of the white and blue motifs used in Oriental pottery.

13

S. VICENTE

MADRE DE DEUS
(The Church of the Mother of God)

This church has a curious history. In 1509 on this spot stood a large church built to contain the remains of the 11,000 virgin martyrs of Cologne, later destroyed in the 1755 earthquake. At that time it was decided to reconstruct the façade as it had originally appeared, drawing upon a painting still preserved in the National Museum of Ancient Art, i.e. the *St. Auta Altarpiece*. In the painting the portal of the church ready to receive the remains of the saint may be seen just as it looked before the earthquake destroyed it, carved in a lovely Manuelian style.

MADRE DE DEUS CHURCH
Interior

This church interior too, with its aisleless nave and upper and lower choruses, is strikingly lovely. Here the azulejos tiles are large-sized panels depicting wide-sweeping landscapes with hunting and pastoral scenes. Glittering with gilded stuccos, the church has a lovely lacunar ceiling of wooden panels set in niches and carved gilded frames.

PRAÇA DO COMÉRCIO

Lisbon's most attractive square, and also one of Europe's most beautiful, is familiarly called by the Portuguese Terreiro do Paço, literally, the Palace Square recalling that once upon a time it was actually the square of the palace before the palace too was destroyed in the great earthquake. As a typical example of the Pombal style, the square has classical, uniform arcading (designed by Eugénio dos Santos) on three sides. The second storey is delicately colored in dark green colors. In the middle of the north side there is a *triumphal arch* designed by the French architect Calmels who also sculpted the allegorical group which crowns it. The arch was executed between 1755 and 1873. The four statues lower down are the work of the Portuguese sculptor V. Bastos and represent four famous Portuguese: Viriato, Nuno Alvares, the Marquis of Pombal, and Vasco da Gama.

In the center of this huge square, measuring 192 by 177 meters, stands the monumental bronze statue depicting King José I. This statue, the work of Machado de Castro who executed it in 1774, was, when it was unveiled, the largest in the world. In this square on February 1, 1908, King Carlos I and his heir, crown prince Luis Filipe, were assassinated.

ELEVADOR SANTA JUSTA

Its construction was begun in 1900 by Raul Mesnier Ponsard, a Portuguese engineer of French origin (1850-1914). Its metal structure unites the lower platform, on Rua do Ouro, to the higher one on the hill of the Carmo. A viaduct built in 1901 links this platform to the Largo do Carmo.

There is a difference in level between the two platforms of 31,92 meters.

In this structure, typical of the period, the use of metal is combined with Neo-Gothic decoration.

THE CARMO

Commissioned by Constable Nuno Alvares Pereira in fulfillment of a vow made for the victory at the Battle of Aljubarrota, it was built by the architects Afonso Gonçalo and Rodrigo Eanes between 1398 and 1423; the church was destroyed in the 1755 earthquake. It was decided never to rebuild it so that everyone would be able to witness the horror and tragedy of that fateful day. And today it is indeed a moving experience to walk down the nave of the Carmo and pass under the soaring ogival arches reaching upwards, but now empty, or to wander about the lawn which has taken over where there was once flooring and which crops up unexpectedly in the most unthinkable places: at the base of the statue of a saint in the pose of blessing, in between the azulejo tiles, and even over a fallen capital. Still standing today are the imposing main chapel, the four ribbed apsidal chapels, and the façade which opens on a porch with huge columns and capitals with figurative and vegetative ornamentation.

THE NATIONAL ASSEMBLY

The St. Bento Palace, originally an antique Benedictine convent, was damaged by fire in 1895. The plan for its reconstruction was designed by the architect Ventura Terra, who conserved the original lines while adding height and introducing sober classical style. The building, now the seat of the Republican Parliament, underwent further changes between 1896 and 1938. In the central body of the façade, where the major transformation took place, the architect placed five arches beneath a balcony of binate columns that support a classical pediment.

The internal arrangement of space derives from a scrupulous study of proportions and functionality.

THE BASILICA DA ESTRÊLA

Erected at the end of the 18th century in imitation of the late Baroque Roman style, the church boasts a sumptuous façade with two orders, bell towers, and a dome over the crossing. The sculptural decoration by Machado de Castro is rather lovely. After having admired the majestic interior, it is a good idea to stroll out into the greenery of the adjoining da Estrela garden which is one of Lisbon's most charming, enhanced by the deep quiet which reigns within.

THE NATIONAL MUSEUM OF ANCIENT ART

The museum was set up in the old palace of the Counts of Alvor following the Exhibition of Decorative Arts in 1882, and was inaugurated in 1883. In the thirties it underwent various transformations including the addition of a large adjoining building, which was to contain the collections of Portuguese painting, Oriental art, ceramics, and religious art.

Porch

This spacious porch containing a small number of select works looks almost bare in its simplicity, almost as if it were an attempt to make us better appreciate the richness of the works to be found upstairs. Chinese and Portuguese pottery, polychrome 15th and 16th century sculpture, Persian carpets, and Della Robbia tondos are the first art works which greet our eyes.

THE NATIONAL MUSEUM OF ANCIENT ART
Chapel of the St. Albert Monastery

At the time when the new annex to the museum was being constructed, the antique convent of St. Albert was demolished, leaving the chapel intact. The chapel was incorporated into the museum, and conserves precious wood intaglios and *azulejos*, typical of 17th and 18th century Portuguese decorative art.

THE NATIONAL MUSEUM OF ANCIENT ART
Crib

This 18th century crib is a typical expression of the simple but fervid faith of the Portuguese people. The crib, which was introduced by St. Francis of Assisi in the 13th century, soon gained great favor and, once having crossed the Italian border, it spread to Austria, France, Spain, and of course Portugal. The landscape surrounding this Nativity scene is highly evocative: there are crags, rocks, and clefts. Moreover, the Nativity does not take place in a humble stable, but rather in a grotto set off by elegant columns. All around there is excitement; the whole scene swarms with people and life, famous and everyday characters. As a result, the religious scene appears in the background, overpowered and submerged by the reality surrounding it.

26

THE NATIONAL MUSEUM OF ANCIENT ART
Portuguese School: *Ecce Homo*

The work of an unknown 15th century artist from the Lisbon School, this *Ecce Homo* is known as the " sphinx of Christian art ". And, in fact, the Christ figure, half hidden in the shroud, really looks like a sphinx with a sphinx's impassiveness and impenetrable mystery of expression.

THE NATIONAL MUSEUM OF ANCIENT ART
Nuno Gonçalves: *The San Vincenzo Altarpiece*

These six panels, which were painted between 1460-1470 and attributed to Nuno Gonçalves, depict the veneration of the city's patron saint. They represent not only masterpieces of Portuguese painting, but also a rare document of Portuguese society in the 15th century.

In fact, besides the saint, the figures depicted include king Afonso V, crown prince João (later king João II), Henry the Navigator, Queen Isabella, Nuno Gonçalves himself as well as knights, monks, fishermen, beggars, and Jews, each figure characterized by subtle psychological insight and painted with an acute feeling for realism.

THE NATIONAL MUSEUM OF ANCIENT ART
Hans Holbein the Elder: *The Virgin and Child with Saints*

The Sacra Conversazione is a highly popular subject in Flemish iconography, and Flemish artists represent it in a host of different ways in various settings. Here the artist has chosen a composition in a single plane which nevertheless penetrates space through the use of the majestic Renaissance architecture dominating the composition. An admirable balance in the composition together with a harmonious blending of colors lends the whole work a feeling of peace and mystical concentration.

THE NATIONAL MUSEUM OF ANCIENT ART
Hieronymus Bosch: *The Temptation of St. Anthony*

This painting was possibly one of the works formerly belonging to the Escorial which was bought by Damiano de Goes, the Portuguese painter, between 1523-1545. The huge triptych was painted by Bosch with special power of inventiveness and color. The painter lets his imagination run wild in his depiction of the temptation of the saint: allegory is the real hero of this work and metamorphosis in its most curious forms takes over each and every element. Nonetheless, in spite of the difficulty involved in making an interpretive reading of the painting, one is always aware of the great balance achieved in the composition and the stupendous tonal cohesion which presides over the whole.

THE DOS COCHES NATIONAL MUSEUM

At the beginning of the 20th century the Portuguese royal house wanted to keep up with the other European reigning houses vying to outdo one another in splendor and luxury, and so they collected a considerable number of old carriages and coaches which proved to be highly superior, not only in quantity but above all in quality, to those which had already been collected in other countries and put on exhibition in museums. Currently, the collection includes 26 carriages, 16 sedans, 4 sedans for processions, 4 sedans for galas, 9 coaches for drives and a host of others.

Joao VI's carriage built in 1824.

Gilded carriages which belonged to José I' built after 1765 with a painting attributed to Cirillo Wolkmar Machado.

French sedan built for the Royal House of Portugal towards the middle of the 18th century.

Gilded carriage which belonged to Queen Marie Anne of Austria, wife of João V, built in Vienna in 1705.

THE DOS JERONIMOS MONASTERY

It was due to a real miracle that this jewel of Manuelian art was spared the day of the 1755 earthquake. Built on order of King Manuel in 1502 after a design by Boytac, the monastery stands on the riverbank from which Vasco da Gama set sail and to which he returned after having opened the way to far-off India and the fabulous East. Despite the different stylistic contributions made by the various architects as they succeeded one another in the construction of the church, the whole gives the feeling of great formal cohesion. The Manuelian style is at its loveliest here, with its exotic depictions and its dreamy recall of the Orient.

Portal

On the right side of the church, the one which faces the square, and farther on, the open sea, one can admire the splendid twin portal with a statue of Henry the Navigator on the dividing pillar. Even the pillars and the buttresses pale beside the exhuberant decoration of the stonework: spires, pinnacles, and niches containing sculpture, but most of all the sea subjects: tangles of knots, shells, and corals. It represents the joyous celebration of a people who sailing the seas had discovered new lands and with them great power and wealth.

THE DOS JERONIMOS MONASTERY

Interior

This church interior is awe-inspiring for its vast proportions and daring architecture, illuminated by a light which, entering from outside, plays upon the delicate ornamentation covering the pillars and vaulting. The vaulting, equally high over the nave and side aisles, is decorated in a delicate pattern of ribs which radiate like the rays of a star over the whole ceiling of the church. The tall, thin pillars are so completely covered with bas-relief carvings that they seem to lose their purpose as bearing members and look as though they have a purely decorative function. It really appears impossible that this architectural design, which looks so very fragile, could have come out of the great earthquake unscathed. And yet the building did not suffer the

least damage, not even in the transept supported by only two pillars!

THE DOS JERONIMOS MONASTERY
The Tombs of Vasco da Gama and Luis de Camões

The tombs of Portugal's most famous and greatest native sons, Vasco da Gama and Luis de Camões, are revealed in the dusky light of the chorus. The former, sailing the high seas, opened up new horizons and discovered new lands, bringing riches from the fabulous and mysterious Orient back to his homeland. The latter in his writings extolled the epoch-making ventures of the former. Camões' poem, **Os Lusiadas** (that is, the sons of Luso or the Portuguese people), embodies the typical Renaissance spirit. Thus Camões may truly be called " the poet of the great discoveries "

THE DOS JERONIMOS MONASTERY

West portal

A number of artists worked on the construction of the church. Thus, besides Boytac who designed it, and João de Castilho, of Spanish descent, we find the signatures of the French master Nicolas Chanterene who accentuated the Renaissance element, as well as Diego de Torralva and Jérome de Rouen who already at the end of the 16th century brought a classical note into the decoration. Chanterene is responsible for this west portal which opens on to what is actually the building's main façade, now half hidden. Built in 1517, the portal has the usual rich, copious ornamentation of freizes and sculpture. In the jambs, the French artist has placed statues of King Manuel with St. Jerome on one side and on the other, Queen Mary with John the Baptist.

THE DOS JERONIMOS MONASTERY
Cloister

It is said that the best time to see the cloister is in the late afternoon when the rays of sun bring out the hot golden hues of the Alcântara stone used to build this master work by Boytac and João de Castilho. The cloister, in the shape of a square measuring 55 meters on each side, has two orders, the lower having double mullioned windows and the upper with spacious arches and single mullioned windows. The decorative exhuberance is almost Oriental: ribs, spiral-shaped reliefs, medallions, and unusual interlacings make it up. Even though the lower loggia is more ornate and the upper one simpler, both blend together in the noble stylistic conception which dominated the creation of the whole.

THE BELÉM TOWER

Lisbon's characteristic symbol, the Belém Tower, majestically rises on the banks of the Tagus where it was built by Francisco d'Arruda between 1515 and 1521. The tower was the white shape that the sailors, from the high masts of their caravels and galleons, searched out as they were concluding their long sea voyages. The curiously shaped towers, the delicate loggias and balconies, the Arabic mullioned windows, and the lovely stone embroidery confer to the tower a Venetian kind of charm which is enhanced by the water lapping on the foundations, while the palm trees shading it make the landscape look almost African.

Nevertheless, all this charm should

not deceive the viewer. In fact, the tower was used as a fortress, as a prison, and as a watch tower too. Prisoners languished in its dungeons while powerful weapons were stored in its dark underground chambers. In the terrace, full of pinnacles and dominated by a splendid Renaissance loggia, the Virgin of Safe Travels looks out towards the Tagus and the open sea, watchful and attentive of the harbor entrance. It is fascinating to visit the inside of the tower furnished with 16th century pieces. Of note is the elegantly proportioned royal bedroom which is topped by beautiful Gothic rib vaulting. From the upper terrace, a glance can take in the entire city, from the slim lines of the ultra modern April 25 Bridge to the mouth of the Tagus which here feeds its waters into the Atlantic Ocean.

THE APRIL 25 BRIDGE

Up till August 1967 (when the bridge was inaugurated) the banks of the Tagus were linked only by ferries. When it was decided that a bridge would be built, the Portuguese wanted it to be beautiful, as modern as could be, and they also wanted it to be the longest suspension bridge in all of Europe. Almost $1^1/_2$ miles long, it rises 230 feet over the Tagus and is supported only by two giant pylons. From the bridge one can admire all of Lisbon spread out below, from the colorful houses of Alfama to the classical façades of Baixa, from the noisy activity of the port to the silence of Belém.

THE STATUE OF "CRISTO REI"

From high above the left bank of the Tagus, it dominates the city spread out at its feet. At night the statue is illuminated like a beacon and is visible from every part of Lisbon.
Inaugurated in 1959, the monument is situated on the south bank of the Tagus, and was erected in fulfillment of a vow made by Portuguese bishops who prayed that their country might escape participation in World War II.

PADRÃO DOS DESCO-BRIMENTOS

(Monument to the Discoveries)

Looking at it from afar, this modern monument (built for the fifth centenary of Henry the Navigator's death), appears to be the prow of a ship about to set sail. Standing on the prow, holding a caravel in his hands and looking straight ahead, is Prince Henry and behind him crowd all the famous and not so famous people of his day who helped him to make his great dreams of voyages and discovery come true. Recognizable are King Manuel, Camões the poet, Nuno Gonçalves the painter, and all the others,

anonymous but equally important, such as soldiers, sailors, pilots, priests, and even women in tears — the widows of the men who left home in search of new worlds to discover and never returned.

PRAÇA DO MARQUÊS DE POMBAL

One reaches this square, known as the **Rotunda,** after walking down the Avenida da Liberdade, a long, tree-shaded avenue, full of palm trees and flower beds perpetually in bloom. Dominating the vast square is a monument erected to the Marquis of Pombal who from on high, a hand buried in a lion's mane, contemplates with deep satisfaction his marvelous work: the tidy city spread out before his gaze, crisscrossed by wide streets and shady avenues. Beyond the square extends the huge Edward VII Park, an elegant and well-kept stretch of gardens.

THE CAMPO PEQUENO

Just as every city on the Iberian peninsula, Lisbon too has its Praça de Touros, or bullfighting arena, an imposing building put up in 1892 in Moorish style. Bullfighting here in Portugal is not, however, the same as the sport practiced in Spain: from 1799 on, it has been forbidden to kill the bull—but this certainly does not mean that the bullfighters and the bullfight are any less exciting. In addition, bullfights in Portugal are held in 18th century costume and the bull is fought by elegant and able picadores who remain mounted on horseback at all times.

THE CALOUSTE GULBENKIAN MUSEUM

The Calouste Gulbenkian Museum was inaugurated in October 2, 1969 to house the rich collection that the Armenian merchant Calouste Sarkis Gulbenkian had donated to Portugal two years before his death in 1955. His last wishes were in fact that the collection he had so lovingly and tenaciously put together in life should not be dispersed upon his death. Thus conceived, the museum is a reflection of the taste, culture, and spirit of several people united by the same purpose: to fully exploit the works of art, not only in terms of their esthetic value, but also as tools of study and culture. With these criteria in mind the modern building was designed

and, in this extremely functional museum layout, the precious art collection may be readily admired.

THE GULBENKIAN MUSEM
Oriental Art

Chinese art occupies an important place in the Gulbenkian collection. The delicate craftsmanship of the objects and their lovely colors, especially blue and white, the most extensively used, were highly appreciated by collectors. Isolated in a showcase before a window look-

ing out on the green of the park, this little ceramic group is one of the loveliest in the collection.

THE GULBENKIAN MUSEUM
French Furniture

Precious French 18th century furnishings are displayed in this gallery in such a real way that a person entering does not feel as though he is entering a museum but rather as if he were stepping into the home of a wealthy French family in which people are really living.

SINTRA

Sintra is located on the northern slope of a granite outcrop bearing the same name and covered with a thick forest of cedars, oaks, ferns, and camellias. Since the clouds blowing from the Atlantic are blocked by the mass of its mountain, Sintra enjoys cool temperatures even during the hottest summers. In fact, the Portuguese royal family, attracted by the beauty of the spot and the healthy air of its environs, chose Sintra for their summer residence. The charms of Sintra with her forest and three castles, have been extolled by a number of great poets including Gil Vincente, Camões and especially Byron in his famous poem **Childe Harold.** The oldest of the three castles is the **Castelo dos Mouros,** which has by now fallen into a state of utter abandon, although its imposing walls still crown the high, rocky cliff which dominates Sintra. Legend would have it that an immense fortune still lies buried beneath the walls, hidden by the Moors during their hasty flight when Afonso Henriques's Crusaders were crowding at their heels. From the top of the towers there is an exceptional view of forests, gardens, and the immense plain below which extends right up to the glitter of the Atlantic Ocean.

THE ROYAL PALACE

Characterized by two enormous cone-shaped chimneys (which were for the kitchen fireplaces), the Royal Palace of Sintra stands in the middle of the village. Its irregular shape is due to the various changes carried out at different times. First, King João I had the central part with its ogival arches and Moorish windows put up and then King Manuel I added on the whole right wing with the exception of the two gigantic chimneys which were put up in the 18th century.

THE ROYAL PALACE
The Stag Room

In few places as inside the Royal Palace can one feel the living presence of a past which seemed so definitely long buried — especially in the Palace's shady patios, in the courtyards smelling of orange trees and the fountains spurting water, and in the huge Persian carpets covering whole drawings rooms with their polished wood floors, or the enameled surface of the azulejo tiles waiting to be lit up in the sun every time the charming Moorish windows are thrown open.... And one of the loveliest rooms of all is the Stag Room. Built at the start of the 16th century it is covered with azulejo tiles illustrating hunting and battle scenes. The curved octagonal dome. which is reminiscent of the ones in Persian mosques is decorated with 72 stags' heads, each one wearing as a badge the arms and names of Portugal's leading families.

THE ROYAL PALACE
The Magpie Room

A curious tale is at the origin of this room's decoration. One day, it happened that King João was caught in the act of kissing one of the ladies in waiting to his wife, Philippa of Lancaster. The king, in an effort to justify himself, proclaimed that the kiss had been bestowed solely **por bem,** i.e. without malice. Nevertheless, this statement of his, even though it calmed down his wife, never managed to put a halt to the ladies' in waiting wagging tongues and rumor spreading. Finally, the king decided to have painted on the ceiling of this room as many magpies as there were lady gossips in his wife's court. Every magpie holds a red rose (symbol of the House of Lancaster), while on the ribbon coming out of each bird's beak are the words POR BEM, the justification that the poor king had repeated over and over again to the bursting point.

THE PENA CASTLE

Eccentric, bizarre, decorated with loggias, turrets, domes, draw bridges, and towers, the Pena Castle stands on the highest peak of the Sintra mountain. It was built by the German prince Ferdinand of Coburg, husband to Queen Maria and cousin to King Ludwig II of Bavaria, the mad king famous for the strange, unsual castles he loved and built.

The building must be taken as a whole, as odd and absurd as you like, but exceedingly quaint and striking. It is a hodgepodge of all the styles possible and imaginable: Arabic, Gothic, Manuelian, Renaissance, Baroque....

The work of erecting the architectural complex was entrusted to a German, Baron Eschwege and, in fact, a statue of Eschwege dressed in armour in the typical pose of a

medieval knight stands on top of a rock projecting out over a precipice. Just how much the prince and his architect let their imaginations run wild may be noted wherever one's glance comes to rest. A typical example is this monstrous being, half human half beast, half fish half tree, which appears as if it had just risen out of some infernal underworld. The figure comes from the arch of one of the portals.

THE PENA CASTLE
Interior

The inside of the palace is just like the outside; a hodgepodge of styles and periods, all jumbled together. And yet there is great fascination emanating from all these rooms, be they bedrooms or ballrooms. One might say that in the furnishings of the castle each period

has given the best of itself: Saxon and Sèvres porcelain, ebany and mother-of-pearl cabinets, alabaster candelabras, carved wood, and enamels. Everything is set out in huge, airy rooms in which practically all the windows look out on the valley, or else open over the rocky precipice on which the castle rises, or else onto the narrow outdoor passageway running around the wall.

QUELUZ

A melancholy air and an atmosphere of slight sadness hang over Queluz, with its faded pink hues, its neat gardens dotted with statuary somewhat corroded by time and weather, and the huge rooms now empty inside the building. Everything evokes the splendor of times gone by, of the luxury and grandeur of the life that once was Queluz. The palace, built between 1758 and 1794, by the Portuguese Mateus Vicente and the Frenchman J. B. Robillon is reminiscent of Versailles in the main section with its receding second storey and in the extensive, one storey wings. But

it is especially in the garden that French influence is most strongly felt. Set out according to the Le Notre model, there are geometric flower beds, grassy carpets, stage sets with odd-looking, sphinx-like statues silently keeping watch above the fountains and pathways winding in and out of the tall hedges. The sumptuous interior is a long chain of huge rooms. One of the most beautiful is the Ambassadors' Hall embellished with mirrors, marbles, and on the ceiling a painting of a concert at the court of King Dom José and other mythological subjects. Another remarkable room is the magnificent Throne Room where the mirrors along the walls reflect the light, splintering it in every way.

CASCAIS

Across the bay is Estoril's rival resort, Cascais, which may be reached on foot by walking along the waterfront. Cascais's quiet and simple charm, its fishermen, old houses, tiny squares with fishnets spread out to dry in the sun, and its quaint narrow streets were discovered by painters who took up residence here, filling the little cafés and typical local restaurants dotting the waterfront with their lively presence.

Today, even though modern hotels have taken the place of the old-style houses, Carcais's characteristic fascination remains intact — the brightly-colored boats docked in the port, the fishermen mending their nets, and the women enjoying the sun on the thresholds of their houses are truly typical.

ESTORIL

If we take the modern highway towards the sea from midtown Pombal Square, after passing a number of quaint little towns, we reach the coast. Here is the resort of Estoril full of people from the international jet set which divides its time between the lovely beach and famous gambling casino before retiring to the exclusive estates hidden away among the greenery.

The wide, palm-shaded avenues, the hibiscuses blooming everywhere, and the park full of tropical and exotic plants annually attract flocks of tourists who find fun and rest in this marvelous setting.

BENFICA

Benfica is one of Lisbon's ancient neighborhoods where splendid villas and beautiful gardens can be seen. The most celebrated one is the mansion of Marquis da Fronteira, built in the 17th century, whose design imitates the Italian Renaissance villas.

INDEX

A Brief History of the City .... *Page* 3
Alafama .... ,, 10
— Casa dos Bicos .... ,, 12
April 25 Bridge .... ,, 44
Basilica da Estrêla .... ,, 22
Belém Tower .... ,, 40
Benfica .... ,, 63
Campo Pequeño .... ,, 47
Cascais .... ,, 60
Cathedral (Sé Patriarcal) .... ,, 6
Church of the Carmo .... ,, 21
Church of São Vicente de Fora .... ,, 12
— Monastery .... ,, 12
— Porch .... ,, 14
Dos Coches National Museum .... ,, 30
Dos Jeronimos Monastery .... ,, 32
— Portal .... ,, 32
— Interior .... ,, 34
— Tomb of Vasco Da Gama and Luis
    da Camões .... ,, 36
— West Portal .... ,, 36
— Cloister .... ,, 38
Elevador Sta. Justa .... ,, 20
Estoril .... ,, 60
Gulbenkian Museum .... ,, 48
— Oriental Art .... ,, 49
— French Furniture .... ,, 49

Madre de Deus Church .... *Page* 15
— Interior .... ,, 16
Miradouro di Santa Luzia .... ,, 11
National Assembly Building .... ,, 22
National Museum of Ancient Art .... ,, 24
— Porch .... ,, 24
— Chapel of the St. Albert
    Monastery .... ,, 25
— Crib .... ,, 25
— Ecce Homo .... ,, 27
— San Vincenzo Altarpiece .... ,, 27
— Virgin and Child with Saints .... ,, 29
— Temptation of St. Anthony .... ,, 29
Padrão dos Descobrimentos .... ,, 46
Pena Castle .... ,, 55
— Interior .... ,, 56
Praça da Figueira .... ,, 6
Praça do Comércio .... ,, 18
Praça do Marquês de Pombal .... ,, 46
Queluz .... ,, 58
Rossio .... ,, 4
Royal Palace .... ,, 50
— Stag Room .... ,, 52
— Magpie Room .... ,, 52
São Jorge Castle .... ,, 8
Sintra .... ,, 50
Statue of Cristo Rei .... ,, 44